What's More Powerful Than You?

Understanding the Greatness Within

Damien S. Johnson

I dedicate my first book to my grandma,

Lillie Bernice Johnson.

FOREWORD

You know how you come across the perfect quote or hear the perfect lines in a song that speak to your heart & hit on exactly what you needed to hear? That's this book!

In today's socially driven society, we can connect with likeminded individuals all over the world or even discover we're close neighbors who just never introduced ourselves. If you're really into a specific genre, such as silent French films, or you want to find local 'yoga with goats' meetups, there are many communities out there for you. This is the joy I have found in connecting with Damien, a person who is of like mind and like heart. As an author, I appreciate the diligence it takes to write a nonfiction book to help others and the painful experiences that inspire us to write. I find that common thread in this book!

There's something special about a person's advice who has been through the experience they're advising on. Everyone knows it's not often fruitful to get relationship advice from a person who has no experience in relationships. In a similar sense, when learning to love yourself, it's best to learn from someone who grew to love themselves now but also had to develop & nurture it through their experiences of not loving themselves then. That's this book!

We have all heard you can't properly love others until you love yourself first. Damien reveals what a person does after they accomplish the contingency, how to properly love others. He learned how valuable it is and more importantly, how this recipe of self-love equates to becoming the best version of who you are. I love this quote by the poet Nizariat, "The finest souls are the ones who gulped pain and avoided making others taste it." On the other side of pain is healing and the gift of love then follows. Again, that's this book!

To sum it up, this is a book that will speak to your heart and will open your mind to many lessons taught in order to achieve self-love, the most important ingredient to true GREATNESS!

L. L. Farris, Author of "The Secret Harvest: The Gardens of Our Lives"

TABLE OF CONTENTS:

INTRODUCTION

My probation officer walked up to me and said, “You’re a very lucky man.” In that moment I had to absolutely agree. Yes, I was successfully let off of my intense probation, even though I did violate curfew several times and had previously tested positive for marijuana so it could have easily gone the other way. I could be doing 3.5 years!

I remember thinking two things; first, I need to figure out my life and secondly, I have some type of purpose much bigger than I ever thought. One summer night in June of 2010, I was watching Poetic Justice and was inspired by Tupac Shakur to become an Actor. This was a dream I had before but was too shy to mention it to anyone. No experience, no connections, complete novice. I studied, researched, made a plan and proceeded to execute. Throughout the years of pursuing acting, I started changing my subconscious mind as the result of extreme challenges that taught me lessons and filled me with wisdom.

From a small country town in North Carolina that has, what people would deem, an enormous pipe dream, I had challenges. I was starting in my later 20s, I'm a father and I have a criminal record. Fast forward to today, where I'm an established actor and model.

I've been in national commercials, shows, and movies. I also coach other actors now.

Not everyone has the same goal as me; some want to pass the state bar to become an attorney or some want to buy their parents a home, or become a millionaire, and some just want to become better individuals in life to positively impact the people they come across. Even though we all have different goals, it's the same recipe for each of us. I had to tap into a power that I was unaware I had that was strong enough to turn a thought into reality. I'm going to say that again, a power that is strong enough to turn a thought into reality.

Upon any success, you are often asked what you did or what was your secret. This leads you to evaluate the changes you implemented on the journey, because trust me, there are certain changes to be made in order to release the full force of the power that all of us possess. That power is greatness.

So as I was self-reflecting, I realized, I started loving myself more and then my choices changed. I forgave myself in order to be forgiven and let go of mental shackles and spiritual blockings. I was aware of who was in my circle, because you are just like the company you keep and they can have an indirect effect on your energy. I was mindful. I created new and better habits, being we're creatures of it, they reflect in and all we do and who we can become. I chose to be happy, which helps internally. I became more thankful, understanding that more abundance comes from appreciation. I also understood I had a purpose and that it carried me when I had those empty, lost moments.

Nobody has all the answers and with this reading, I just simply share things that have proven to work for me in my pursuit of becoming my greatest version. Whether you take the whole thing or a piece and can add it to your routine, and it helps then, then that's a win for the both of us.

Now that we've gotten that out the way, let's dive into these chapters and help you understand your greatness within!

1.LOVE

Let us start at the root of it all. Love! This is the highest frequency in the universe. The famous quote "loves conquers all" could not be any truer. Do me a favor, close your eyes, and just think of the person or people you love the most for 10 seconds! Now, do you see that feeling you get? That energy, warmth and delight that emits from your heart and overwhelms your body is true love. Now I have a question. When you close your eyes and think about your own self, do you have that same feeling? If so, wonderful; if not, why?

Before we can love anyone the correct

way, we must first love ourselves. There has not been anyone you have been with more, day in and day out, for all your life, than yourself. So why not love yourself to the highest magnitude?

Many times, we can give and give to others and yet, forget to pour into ourselves. Whether it be pampering yourself, affirmations, setting aside a day just for yourself, or looking in the mirror and smiling at God's divine masterpiece, we should always remember that when we show love to ourselves, we are showing God we appreciate his one of a kind creation. Because that is certainly what you are, one of a kind! Loving yourself will show and attract! By that, I mean because when you are doing it properly it, will come with a glow and become an infectious attraction. When I speak on the subject that means mentally, spiritually, and physically. Let us touch on each one individually.

From the physical aspect, what are you eating? Drinking? Are you working out? Do you smoke? These and more play vital roles in your physical health. Have you noticed when people get a brand-new car, they go the extra mile to take care of it? Washing and waxing it, vacuuming it, keeping the windows clean, keeping the oil changed, changing the breaks, keeping all the fluids full of the

CORRECT fluids. Some days they don't want to even drive it. Why? Because they want to keep it in the best condition possible, inside, and out, and it also shows they CARE.

If your body and the things you allow into it were your car, how many more miles do you think you have? Is it still like new, or does it have dents, scratches, torn leather? Is there trash everywhere? Will it crank on its first try or do have to wait a while, get a jump or are you going to need to push it? We shouldn't wait until our cars are on E to get gas, so let's not wait for our bodies to be on E before we try to improve. Exercise is a staple but also a balanced diet including fresh fruits and vegetables, limited meats and a lot water is ideal. I'm not suggesting going and lifting the whole gym the first day. 20 minutes of physical activity a day will do for most. Walking is great for the heart and yoga is excellent as well. Set daily small goals. For example, if you did 5 pushups today, go for 6 tomorrow, and so on.

Write down and keep track of your progress and see how far you came. Same thing with food. Set daily goals, remember the world wasn't built in one day, so it will take time and may seem hard but hard doesn't equal impossible. When you complete your goals, you'll feel accomplished, start to feel better, and look better which brings confidence and that only helps YOU! Getting rid of crippling habits, such as smoking and excessive drinking, will improve the heart tremendously. Again, it's all about loving yourself enough to do it. People may say, "I don't have time", but I'm a firm believer that we can make time for things we want and/or love which should definitely be ourselves.

Secondly let's discuss the mental aspect. What are you listening to? Who are you listening to and are you mindful of what you are saying about yourself? What are your thoughts, and do you believe them? We must learn to reprogram our mind, our habits, and in reality, our subconscious mind.

Our subconscious mind is what is used to do things we don't think of, such as breathing, walking, etc. It knows no variation between what's reality and what's not. So, things that are thought and said repetitively are soaked into there with no choice but to manifest. Literally! The pledge of allegiance isn't something said daily or to some it's something that hasn't been said since elementary school but I'm sure you can say it, word for word, still till this day. Why? It was embedded into your subconscious.

Muhammad Ali once said he was calling his self the greatest before he knew it, subconsciously he was programming his mind and we all know how decorated his career was and till this very day he is still revered to be the greatest boxer ever in most circles. So, if you're waking up with thoughts like "this is going to be a bad day", then guess what? You're absolutely right, it will be. It will seem as if everything goes wrong after you make that statement.

Again, the subconscious doesn't know the difference between what's real or what's not, so it just goes by what's said. I challenge you to wake up and say, "today will be amazing" or "this will be the best day ever" and see the difference. The music & people we listen to can affect us tremendously mentally, so we want to keep it uplifting and positive, no matter the genre or topic. I'm often listening to inspiring music and even motivational speeches when I wake up, on the way to work and/or before I go to bed. Things that make you feel inspired and great! You deserve greatness in all capacities because you are just that GREAT! Negative thoughts affect the body as well. Severe sickness can derive from toxic words and thoughts, aches and pains can occur from constant negativity. So, keeping everything positive is vital. The love for yourself should and will keep you mindful of all of the things that could affect your mentality.

Lastly, the spiritual. Now I respect all religions and dare not judge anyone for their personal preference, but we can agree that they all have one thing in common. There is one creator above everything. Some believe he is in the sky but in reality, that's far from the truth. The most high dwells INSIDE of each and every one of us, so when you're loving yourself, you're also loving the most high. It's difficult to hear the words from God and receive the supreme love when your spirit is dirty, mental cloudy and physically lacking. Meditation is something that always helps me.

I remember watching an Oprah Winfrey interview and she stated it wasn't until she sat still that she heard God give purpose and direction. That and/or prayer can feed your spirit. Don't feel pressured to feel you have to talk a whole chapter to the most high. Sometimes I just say, "Thank you for everything". Trusting your God will alleviate so much so called "stress" (a word and thought I despise). A lot of times we try to fight spiritual battles alone. Those battles are meant for the creator. Why stress when you serve a God who made the land, water, and the whole universe! With that type of power, nothing can stop you!

Another thing that's overlooked is that you have to be mindful of who you allow in your bed. SPIRITS DO TRANSFER and this will always affect your spirit. Remember some spirits aren't of GOD! ALL of this is pivotal in improving love for yourself, in turn helping create your greatest version and also love others. Learn to love your flaws as well as your perfections. They're yours, and there is only one person like you in this universe. You are special! You are loved and if you feel nobody loves you, know the creator does and so do I! Say this with me: I AM LOVED. Repeat it every day and say it with force and velocity each time. I would recommend you do it in the mornings as part of your morning routine and before bed!

Key points/checklist

2.FORGIVE YOURSELF

We're often taught to forgive others, as well as ask for forgiveness from whomever we feel we should and deserves it. Honestly, the forgiveness in any aspect isn't so much for the other person as it is for yourself. It eliminates feelings of guilt, resentment, amongst other things and that improves your mind, bringing you a peace. To some it's hard but even the most selfish can admit it's necessary. I pose this question, as much as you have forgiven, because I'm sure at some point you've forgiven someone, have you forgiven YOURSELF? We all make mistakes, it's a part if this thing called life. Without the mistakes, you wouldn't learn. It also helps build character if you don't make the same mistakes.

You ever heard someone always revert back to their past, no matter how long ago it was and say "Had I not" or "If I didn’t" or even say "things would be so different if"? Truth may be within all those sayings, but the fact will forever remain, it's the past and it's over now. Sometimes the people you ask for forgiveness, have forgave and moved on with their lives while some of us hold on for days, weeks, and sadly, years. Some parents haven't forgiven themselves for having kids at a young age; some men and women haven't forgiven themselves for failed marriages; and this goes back to our mental health from the previous chapter, and as I stated in that chapter, the mental will affect the physical.

We cannot go forward, by looking back and if you do, the chances of you falling on your face is inevitable. Forgiving your own self gives you a sense peace and clarity along this long journey called life. People forgive others all the time just on the basis of their love for them, and that takes me back to self-love where we have to love our ourselves enough to say "it's ok, I forgive you" and then let it go; no matter how difficult, just let it go! Don't just say it and not follow through because you'll only be hurting yourself and we love ourselves too much for that, right? You're too special.

You can take on new challenges when you're free from any baggage or mental shackles. The universe already throws the kitchen sink at us every day, don't help it. To be forgiven, we must forgive and that includes ourselves. Be your own best friend. I'm sure you would find it in your heart to forgive and go on with the relationship with someone you have profound love for like a best friend, even husband or wife in some aspect. I just want you to understand how great you are, how important you are. Someone out there loves you and we know one person who should, and that's the person in the mirror.

Speaking of mirrors, I have an exercise I would encourage. Now the deeper the skeletons you have, the harder this may seem just because it will take a lot for a person to face them head on but it's all a part of being a greater version for yourself. Remember, hard doesn't equate to impossible. I would like you to go in your bathroom or bedroom, anywhere there is a mirror (you can even use a handheld), lock the door, look yourself directly in the eyes and say aloud what it is you forgive yourself for, and I mean everything. Be sure to keep eye contact, say each and everything that's held such a grasp on your mind until the slate is clean.

If you began to reflect in your mind or started to cry, it's ok, it's just you letting all of that guilt, resentment, and embarrassment flow out of the dark buried place it once dwelled for however long. It takes a big person to forgive others and a bigger person to forgive themselves. Don't rush through the exercise, take deep breaths in between each thing you're forgiving yourself for. This is a personal intervention. BE HONEST in all that you say. After you finish, leave it all there, it's now over, no need to bring it back up and/or dwell on it.

You forgave yourself! Be excited for accomplishing it! Be excited for what's to come! You will be amazed how much dead weight, that's never acknowledged, can block your blessings. How much it can hold your true potential down like a boat anchor. Now that you understand the sovereignty of that, let's look outward and revisit forgiving others. This also lines up with the law of karma, which in a nutshell says that what goes around comes around. Being upset or holding a grudge with another person is you dimming your own light. It's very possible to ask anyone for forgiveness but it's also possible that it may not be granted because you haven't let go of an issue with someone else.

I'm a firm believer that time heals all wounds, we just don't need that wound being so deep you need surgery. Compassion is something we have inside for others, no matter how much we mask it. The most high said, we're made in his image and we know how deep his passion runs so again, it's in us. We don't want to be forced to show it under the wrong circumstances. For example, I've seen people have an issue with someone that gets hurt badly, loses a loved one or even passes away. I can say, wanting to forgive someone when they are in a casket is a feeling that will leave way more than a sour taste in your mouth and then from that, a snowball of " I wishes". Which can take you back to a feeling of guilt and you're back to not wanting to forgive yourself for it.

You start to realize some things aren't as serious as we make it out to be and whatever feelings you had to make you come to an unforgiving state, was just a temporary, emotional frame of mind. A lot of times we just need a moment to cool down, how long of a moment is your discretion but once your emotions subside, think about everything in a whole and make the correct decision. As I stated before, the forgiving is not so much for the other person, its more so for you, and it will help you along this journey to become your greatest version. So, when your faced with a similar situation in the future, stop for a second and think.

Is it really that serious?

Why did they do what they did?

Have I ever been forgiven for something I did that was frowned upon? Having mercy will ultimately bring the same and intertwined in that mercy, is love.

Key points/checklist

3.YOUR CIRCLE

"You are who you're with the most", ever heard that? How about "birds of a feather, flock together". These are just two of the many variations that speaks on the company you keep. I personally love the quotes; they hold so much truth. Whomever you allow in your circle can directly, as well as indirectly, have an effect on your wellbeing in all aspects. If you're around 5 millionaires every day, it's almost like you have no choice but to become the sixth. Hang around 5 "broke people", then you have no choice but to become the 6th in that regard. You become an observant slave to their habits, which over time can easily become your own.

Our bodies are balls of energy, and whatever energy you're around can transfer to you, positive or negative. It's critical that you're well aware of the energy that's in your space at ALL times. You ever been somewhere and someone with a happy, positive energy walks in and the whole atmosphere in the room changes? They ultimately leave and you feel better, happier, and more vibrant. That is what's called an energy transfer. (That's the type energy you want not only to be around but also exude) The same way that person's positive energy transferred to you, you can do just the same and would want to do the same.

Aside from being an author, I'm also an actor and a lot of roles I ended up landing was on the account of my positive, optimistic, upbeat spirit. Of course, my talent had something to do with it as well but I've been in rooms where there was far better talent than myself and I still ended up getting the role because of the energy I spread throughout the room. Not everyone can relate to that particularly so before then, when I had job interviews, I can assure you my energy got me the job. Even with other candidates who were more qualified or had similar experience, the deal breaker was the energy I exuded. At times, the hiring manager would want to know more about me personally, even offering to grab some coffee or play some golf with them at the course.

Being inspired by the people you're around is not always a promising thing, depending on character and inspirations can be positive as well as negative, depending on circumstances. For example, if you're around drug dealers all the time and you're in a pickle financially, you may be inspired to do the same. If you're around drug users and feeling down or helpless, you may be inspired to just take a hit to feel better. Not saying that you will but the chances are heightened, with or without peer pressure. This reminds me of when I was younger and did something out of character. My excuse to my parents was "Well, my friend did it" and my parent's typical reply was “Well, if your friend jumped off a bridge, would you do that too?”. The same philosophy applies when we’re older.

I would like you to look at your closest friends, look at their profession, how they treat people, how they speak about others, their family as well as themselves.

Do they speak words of positivity, words that uplift?

How do you feel once you see them up until when they leave?

Do you hate to see them coming?

How do they INSPIRE you?

You want a circle of friends that make you a better person in all aspects, ones that have your best interest at heart. Not people who just tell you want you want to hear. Iron sharpens iron so that calls for sharp and strong friends. We don't want "plastic knife" friends, ones that bend and break under the smallest of pressure. We need the strength of that iron. Life has its fair share of tests, some in which you'll need a solid team effort, a strong support system you may say, people to pull you up when life hits you with something that can bring you to your knees...from the day we learn what friends mean, a lot of our best moments in life involve people we consider friends. You want friends that never settle, ones that bring the best out of you and challenge you daily to become a better human being. Friends that speak life into you.

Now on the other side of the spectrum, we want to avoid people who are the total opposite. Ones who don't mean us well, people that display envy, have hate/anger inside, liars, gossipers. Some people would ask, how can we tell? Pay attention to everything, especially the energy and your gut instinct. The gut or consciousness never lies. Some say that instinct is actually GOD communicating to us. The particular traits, that if named, aren't fit for a healthy and trustworthy friendship, in turn the relationship will always be stagnant or nonexistent throughout the minimal good times that may come from it.

There are friendships that have been going for years and years and nothing positive has come from it. People often look at a friendship different than a relationship but, in all actuality, it's just a different level of a relationship. So just how the rules apply for a spouse, the same can be applied to your friends. At times we follow our heart and not our minds. You may have grown a certain amount of care for that person but deep down you KNOW they aren't helping you improve to become your greatest version. I pose the same question as I did in the previous chapter, how much do you love yourself?

Do you care for that person more than your own wellbeing?

Do you find yourself pouring more into the friendship and not getting anything back in your cup?

Are they adding value or taking away value?

These are crucial questions you have to ask in your process of being the greatest version. Certain people with certain energies can block blessings. Even if you were to get a blessing, it could be relatively small in comparison to what you could have received. Remember some friends are around for seasons, not for a lifetime. It should never be a struggle with any type of friendship. It should be effortless. That’s called being in the flow. Just like when you see a stream, certain rocks are side by side and the water in the stream flows smoothly throughout. That's how friendships and life should be. If you were to drop a boulder in the middle of a flowing stream, we'd agree that the trajectory would change, and enough boulders can stop the flow of water completely. The rocks that are side by side and work together are the friends who exhibit support and guidance, not interfering with your direction, but the boulders represent the friends who you don't need, the ones who delay or can even stop your growth. Plain and simple "just in the way".

Now let's sit back and ask the question of what type of friend you are - are you the rocks or the boulder? Do you inspire your peers? Do you light up the room or dim it? The same friend you would want to have in your circle is the same type of friend you would want to be. You attract whatever you exude out. Always keep that in mind in your journey.

Key points/checklist

4.HABITS

Self-care is essential if you love and care for those around you. When was the last time you took an hour just to wander around the shops aimlessly or watch a movie in your pajamas with a cup? Alone, relaxed and just chill-out time for you; time to do something you love. When did you last take time to forget the job stress before you burn out? Are you spending long hours at work, coming home, cooking dinner, cleaning up and collapsing in front of the TV just to fall asleep and do the whole thing over again the next day?

Now that lack of self-care is a recipe for stress, anxiety, depression, and burnout, in that order. In our fast world, we need to find the time to slow down, relax, have some fun, meditate, journal, take a bubble bath, spend some time with the kids and switch off. Take time to empower ourselves and keep those stress levels in check. Having time alone to do what you love is an important part of this. No matter how wonderful your family life or relationship is, no two people are alike and what you love to do may not be what your partner loves. So, if he or she wants to go skiing while you shop the whole day, do so. That separateness in your relationship will make for a better relationship, not separate you. It will relax you both and give you time to bring new and exciting experiences and conversations to the table. Also, in that time, turn off the phone, the computer and do something creative. Paint, meditate, cook, read, or start a new hobby you have always wanted to try.

Perhaps you're feeling frustrated and impatient. Take some time out to journal how you feel. No-one will read it but you. An important part of self-care is to be able to express yourself and not be overwhelmed. Get it out of your mind and your heart and onto that paper. You are not writing a novel, so it doesn't even have to make sense. Just let it spill out and write what you feel — good or bad. Perhaps there are some things you need to let go of, so start writing a list titled as "I let go of …". Or maybe there's someone you need to forgive. Write them an imaginary letter to forgive them — for your self-care, to make you feel better. They will never see the letter. You can keep it or destroy it but gets those emotions out of your system. Your emotional and mental self-care is just as important as the physical. Take time out to heal those old wounds causing emotional pain.

Maybe your way to take care of yourself is to make a bubble bath, sit in a sauna or even take a swim. Why not set up a routine with some oil pulling to clear out the toxins in your mouth and follow that with some dry body brushing? Once you get used to doing this, you can make it part of your self-care daily routine. Oil pulling is best done with organic, virgin, cold-pressed coconut oil. Start with a few minutes, with just two teaspoons until you build up to the required amount. Body brushing improves circulation, exfoliates dead skin, helps with lymph drainage, and detoxifies your skin. You can research both of these topics to find out how to do them properly.

Your emotional and mental self-care is just as important as the physical. Take time out to heal those old wounds causing emotional pain. Self-care here can take the form of reading an inspirational book, some new input, practicing yoga, tai chi, or Pilates to move the energy around and undo some of those energy blockages. Focus on your breath and breathe out your frustration and anger while breathing in peace and acceptance. Notice how you breathe during the day and if it's in the top part of your chest, realize that you are stressed. Make your breathing just that little bit deeper. Imagine you are breathing into below your naval. That is where your second energy center is and the center of your creativity. It will calm you and sharpen your mind, plus provide many other benefits such as releasing negative emotions and stress. Add to this some stretching and gentle exercises to really open up your chest.

When you wake up in the mornings, have a good, long stretch in bed. Even if you have aches and pains, you can use the bed to support you while you gently move and stretch out those muscles. If you aren't very supple, then do some early morning stretches out of bed, before your shower, to wake your body up. Move your energy around by grounding yourself as part of your daily self-care routine. You will find you are more focused and calmer.

Get in touch with the earth — walk barefoot on some grass in your back garden or go for a walk on the beach if you can, before breakfast. Grounding will bring your energy back in balance and the negative ions from the earth and sea will help discharge some of those free radicals that cause inflammation and make us ill. The earth has the power to heal us if we let it. Grounding can improve all areas of your life.

Even if you implement just a few of these suggestions, your level of self-care will increase. That will take the pressure off your anger, anxiety, and stress. It will make you a happier person and that will flow on to the people around you — those you love and care for will notice a difference. So, if you have a lot of responsibility in your life and people that depend on you, it is vital that you practice some self-care, for them and for yourself.

Key points/checklist

5.THANKFULNESS

I AM THANKFUL

Appreciative, grateful, thankful! This aligns with the law of__________.... A lot of times we tend to get frustrated at the place we are in our career, or where our bank account is, where our love life is, that we don't have a new vehicle even something as small as how many shoes we have. I myself have been guilty of that on numerous occasions. I had to realize something though. I was too busy looking forward, and/or being frustrated with having x pair of shoes that I wasn't thankful that I even had 1 pair. My father told me a long time, there is always someone out there that would appreciate the things you take for granted.

I pose these questions - how can we be blessed with the car of our dreams if we can't appreciate the car we already have? How can we be blessed to move through the ranks if we're complaining about the position we're in now, and how can we be blessed with the woman or man of our dreams if we didn't appreciate the one that was sent before? If the most high can't see your appreciation of the $100 they blessed you with, there's no chance the most high will bless you with $1000. I'm sure if you were in their shoes, you'd agree.

Now back to that car. It may not be the prettiest car, but does it run? It may not have all the bells and whistles that ideally, we all wouldn’t mind but does the AC work? Even if the AC doesn’t, does the window roll down? We have to train our minds to not focus on what we don't have so that we forget to be thankful for all that we do. I’ll go a bit deeper and more personal.

A lot of times, I see kids who just oppose whatever it is our parents want for us because they don’t see the bigger picture. Nowadays, I’ve seen a dramatic rise in disrespect towards mothers and fathers. It comes to a head when something tragic happens. Your parents get hurt, fall ill or even worse, pass away. Then comes regret of how we didn't appreciate and make the most of the time they were here. Things that were said that can’t be taken back haunt our minds. Times where we said "I’ll just call back tomorrow" are easy to say until you can't call back anymore.

I don't look at being thankful as an option, it’s a must, a definite requirement to me. Yes, for advancement but as you can see, it goes deeper than that. For example, you’re making $10 per hour now, but just know there is someone making $7, and someone else has no income whatsoever.

When I was around 23, I had 2 cars and a nice size bank account, but I wasn't appreciative. People needed rides and I'd brush them off; I drove recklessly and spent money the same way. One of my biggest mistakes is how I stopped acknowledging the most high who put me in position to even have a car... I'd say I was on my high horse for about 3 months and the end result, I had not even a fourth of what was in my account, blew one engine and totaled the other car. Now, I'm the one asking for rides and guess what? I was getting brushed off just as I did to others.

It was months and months before I was halfway back in that position. I spent more time working to get back in a stable position than I did actually being in the that position. I will admit it was nobody's fault except my own but once I got it, my eyes were more widespread, and I appreciated the smaller things. The most high giveth and the most high taketh away.

I'd encourage you to just sit back and think about what you do have. When, or if, you pray when communicating with your GOD, just say thank you for it all. Write down the things you're thankful for and hang it on your refrigerator or bathroom mirror or maybe even somewhere in your car. It will keep you grounded and show your appreciation. For the ones who do pray, it's easy to get caught up in asking and asking the most high for things but I'd like to recommend during your next prayer, or even just when you reflect, just simply say thank you for it all! That in itself is so powerful!

How do you feel when you do something from your heart for someone and they say thank you? Makes you feel good, right? The same thing applies when you're praying, reflecting or meditating. With that show of genuine appreciation, you wouldn't mind helping that person out again and even on the next time, giving more! There's so much to be appreciative for that I don't feel there's room for complaining. If you feel different, I can give a few examples that will open your eyes a bit more and put things in a clearer perspective.

You’re reading this book now but somewhere, there are blind individuals wishing they could do the same, let alone see the beauty of a sunrise or sunset, the beauty of a butterfly, or the colors of a rainbow.

You’re subconsciously breathing right now but someone is on a breathing machine, getting aided to breath. Maybe someone took their last breath yesterday or maybe even while you've been reading this chapter. You've taken two breaths just reading that last sentence.

You likely had the financial means to obtain this book and it may not seem like much to you but to someone who has nothing, wondering where they will get the funds to feed their kids. The same amount is a dire amount to some for food and yet, a luxury for others to get some literature.

Those three examples alone are enough to make one think hard. Even while I'm writing, I'm thinking of more ways I can show my appreciation. The world in many ways is a revolving door, it all comes back around.

Key points/checklist

6.HAPPINESS

I CHOOSE HAPPINESS

Who doesn’t like being happy? Honestly, who? Not sure about you but I can't think of one individual. Even the meanest of people wouldn't turn down happiness. *Saying this word, happiness, repetitively aloud gives you a feeling*

I’m one of the most optimistic people you'll ever meet. My cup is always full. I just refuse to let outside forces steal my joy, whether it’s people or circumstances that are beyond my control. Happiness is a choice. Now, life is going to bring its share of ups and downs. That's inevitable, but it's not the things that happen to you but more so the reaction we give to it and if we allow it to have power over us. Remember energy transfers and I feel you should often ask yourself, am I observing the situation accurately or am I projecting how I feel into what's happening??

A quite simple example I see often happens at fast food restaurants when someone gets their order back and there has been a mistake. I have seen some people in such a fit of rage that you would think that they had been poisoned. I understand on top of being hungry, you want something you spent your hard-earned money on to be correct but just observe the situation in a whole. Before you become upset or frustrated, which are opposites of happiness think. Hey, people make mistakes. Just that simple. Now think, how can me being furious help ME in this situation?

You love yourself, right? Look out for yourself at all costs! You are royalty! One of my favorite lyrics is from Ex-Factor by Lauryn hill. "It could all be so simple, but you'd rather make it hard". NOBODY has more authority over how you feel than yourself. Your happiness is your own choice. By the same token, you consent to your unhappiness as well. I often think of just how thankful I am of things.

That's enough in itself. Think about some of your most proud and happy moments. Those type of feelings never go away. That kind of happiness is a feeling that you would want every day, especially over being upset or sad. Strive for it. As soon as you awake, make conscious choices to grow and secure your happiness. The type of music I listen to helps me, as well as books, doing things for others, and exercising. Accomplishing goals, hourly, daily, or even yearly.

I do want you to understand, people you are dealing with can bring unneeded, unhappy energy. Keep them away from you! I scream that from the highest mountain top.

Understand no matter what they do or what they say, it's your choice of how you will react to it. That is YOURS!! Please do not torture yourself.

Certain individuals tend to relate objects to happiness or even people. As if their happiness relies on having those objects or being with that person. That could not be any further from the truth when it comes to you choosing to be happy. It is as simple as making a choice; discipline and dedication play within that too, but the point right now is you making a sound choice. Do not allow temporary emotions to rob you of the happiness you deserve. Change your viewpoint, how you assess the situation.

For example, let's imagine you have $500 and you had to spend $350 to get a repair part for your car. Some would complain about buying the part, and the $350 they had to give up, as opposed to being happy about getting the necessary part to fix your car. Your day will go smoother thinking this way. See how that works. Now you're happy and thankful, so within that comes more abundance and positivity. All behind a choice to be happy, look at how so much more comes about! Your energy transfers so let us transfer the positive, happy feelings.

Another thing, you never know when your time will come. Truly live like it is your last day because at some point in time, it will be. So, in the words of Bobby Mcferrin, "don't worry, be happy"!

Key points/checklist

7. MINDFULNESS

I AM MINDFUL

It’s a busy world. You fold the laundry while keeping one eye on the kids and another on the television. You plan your day while listening to the radio and commuting to work, and then plan your weekend. But in the rush to accomplish necessary tasks, you may find yourself losing your connection with the present moment—missing out on what you are doing and how you are feeling. Did you notice whether you felt well-rested this morning or that forsythia is in bloom along your route to work?

The cultivation of mindfulness has roots in Buddhism, but most religions include some type of prayer or meditation technique that helps shift your thoughts away from your usual preoccupations toward an appreciation of the moment and a larger perspective on life. Increasing your capacity for mindfulness supports many attitudes that contribute to a satisfied life. Being mindful makes it easier to savor the pleasures in life as they occur, helps you become fully engaged in activities, and creates a greater capacity to deal with adverse events.

By focusing on the here and now, many people who practice mindfulness find that they are less likely to get caught up in worries about the future or regrets over the past, are less preoccupied with concerns about success and self-esteem, and are better able to form deep connections with others. If greater well-being is not enough of an incentive, scientists have discovered that mindfulness techniques help improve physical health in a number of ways. Mindfulness can: help relieve stress, treat heart disease, lower blood pressure, reduce chronic pain, improve sleep, and alleviate gastrointestinal difficulties.

In recent years, psychotherapists have turned to mindfulness meditation as an important element in the treatment of a number of problems, including depression, substance abuse, eating disorders, couples' conflicts, anxiety disorders, and obsessive-compulsive disorder. There is more than one way to practice mindfulness, but the goal of any mindfulness technique is to achieve a state of alert, focused relaxation by deliberately paying attention to thoughts and sensations without judgment. This allows the mind to refocus on the present moment. All mindfulness techniques are a form of meditation.

Basic mindfulness meditation

- Sit quietly and focus on your natural breathing, or just on a word, or “mantra”, that you repeat silently. Allow thoughts to come and go without judgment and return your focus back to your breath, word, or mantra.
- Body sensations – Notice subtle body sensations, such as an itch or tingling, without judgment and let them pass. Notice each part of your body in succession from head to toe.
- Sensory – Notice sights, sounds, smells, tastes, and touches. Name them “sight,”

"sound," "smell," "taste," or "touch" without judgment and let them go.

- Emotions – Allow emotions to be present without judgment. Practice a steady and relaxed naming of emotions: "joy," "anger," "frustration." Accept the presence of the emotions without judgment and let them go.
- Urge surfing – Cope with cravings (for addictive substances or behaviors) and allow them to pass. Notice how your body feels as the craving enters. Replace the wish for the craving to go away with the certain knowledge that it will subside.

Mindfulness can be cultivated through mindfulness meditation, a systematic method of focusing your attention. You can learn to meditate on your own but I've learned that many types of meditation primarily involve concentration—repeating a phrase or focusing on the sensation of breathing, allowing the parade of thoughts that inevitably arise to come and go.

Concentration meditation techniques, as well as other activities such as tai chi or yoga, can induce the well-known relaxation response, which is very valuable in reducing the body's response to stress.

Mindfulness meditation builds upon concentration practices.

Here's how it works:

- Go with the flow. In mindfulness meditation, once you establish concentration, you observe the flow of inner thoughts, emotions, and bodily sensations without judging them as good or bad.
- Pay attention. You also notice external sensations such as sounds, sights, and touch that make up your moment-to-moment experience. The challenge is not to latch onto a particular idea, emotion, or sensation, or to get caught in thinking about the past or the future. Instead, you watch what comes and

goes in your mind and discover which mental habits produce a feeling of well-being or suffering.

- Stay with it. At times, this process may not seem relaxing at all, but over time it provides a key to greater happiness and self-awareness as you become comfortable with a wider and wider range of your experiences.
- Practice acceptance. Above all, mindfulness practice involves accepting whatever arises in your awareness at each moment. It involves being kind and forgiving toward yourself.

Some tips to keep in mind:

- Gently redirect. If your mind wanders into planning, daydreaming, or criticism, notice where it has gone and gently redirect it to sensations in the present.
- Try and try again. If you miss your intended meditation session, simply start again.
- By practicing accepting your experience during meditation, it becomes easier to accept whatever comes your way during the rest of your day. Mindfulness is the practice of purposely focusing your attention on the present moment—and accepting it without judgment.

Mindfulness is now being examined scientifically and has been found to be a key element in stress reduction and overall happiness. I focused more on meditation this chapter because it's the most needed and helpful here.

Key points/checklist

8. PURPOSE

I HAVE PURPOSE

I cannot count the times I heard someone say they never imagined they would be ____________________________.

You can fill in the blank because I am sure you have heard it many times yourself. We all have a divine purpose. You are no accident! I will be the first to admit that I had to deal with selfishness of the body in this physical realm. Never forget we are really spirits dwelling inside these bodies. You are the driver of the car and your body is the actual car. You are not Ironman; you are the man or woman inside the suit.

As I stated before, nobody has been around you more than YOURSELF, making it very easy to walk to the beat of your own drum but forget that you are here for a higher powers divine purpose. You can still attain WHATEVER you desire but the true purpose will continue to whisper in your ear. Well, that's at least how it starts until after a while, it gets louder and louder, until you eventually have to pay attention to it.

Now once you acknowledge that whisper echoing from your heart, you can make the choice to either follow it or ignore it. If you choose the second option, I can almost guarantee you will always feel as if something is missing or unable to fill this empty feeling.

You can believe that there's something else you should be doing but if you tell yourself a lie long enough, eventually you will believe it. I can almost assure that you are not here to pay bills and die.

Many things we chase are not even real or aids to our purpose. What do I mean? You ever hear the expression that says, "I've never seen a U-Haul behind a hearse"? Yes, money is essential to survival in this world unfortunately, but you cannot be a slave to it. Work hard to feed your soul and gain more understanding of who you truly are. Pay more attention to the lessons you have went through in life. Nothing is coincidental. Every moment is shaping you for who you are to become to live in your truth.

Lessons will always come; they will repeat until you get it and even then, you will still encounter more. Your purpose can be your connection to something larger, something that will allow you to make your mark on the world, to truly make a difference. Still, your WHY might be different and you need this as your anchor just in case things get a little foggy. To find it, just answer this question: Why do you want to find your purpose in life?

Write down or remember whatever comes up. Whatever it is, cherish it, and remember that nothing is too far left field. Use this as a driving force to help you with your discipline.

Now I have some affirmations that will help along this journey.

You'll need a pen and piece of paper, a working memory, and the drive to uncover what you set out to find. That's it—you're ready to set off. Before we go, there are a few things you will need to embrace beforehand. Think of these items as the underlying code of conduct for your journey. Write down:

- I welcome the hard work and tiresome effort it will take to unearth my life's great work.

- I know my purpose might not be directly obvious, but I will put in the time to find it.
- I believe finding my purpose is entirely possible.
- I know that finding my life's purpose may lead to some drastic (positive) changes.
- I know that finding my life's purpose will leave me with the power to shape my own destiny.

Once you've let the above affirmations settle, add that to your why and you'll be more equipped. These are powerful and become even more powerful when the turbulence of life comes into play. Your tools are sharpened, and your mind is prepped. I might add that prayer and meditation is really helpful for me. I say prayers as my way of communicating and then I sit in meditation as a way of listening. I would urge you to look up some meditation classes, books or even apps on your phone.

You've come farther than most people ever but as a warning I may add that you don't need to fret when you run into initial resistance; a pervading fear, a fear of the unknown you might face will likely be your internal beliefs. They might try to stop you in your tracks or tell you that you are crazy for trying to find your purpose in the first place. They might say harsh things like "you don't deserve to have a purpose", or "you'll never find what you're looking for".

What you must know is that this inner dialogue is not true, it is more afraid than you are. Its main goal is to keep you comfortable. To combat your inner dialogue, you have to first realize it's happening. When you start to actually pay attention to the thoughts as they're spiraling, then they lose their power. They get their evil force by operating below the scenes, so when you shine a spotlight of awareness upon them, they lose their control over you. Once you are familiar with these inner thoughts, it's easier to overcome.

Try this on for size: When you have come across a belief that is threatening to stop your journey for purpose, take a breath and look it square in the eye, then act anyway. This will teach you to develop your courage muscle, and its heart-centered courage will give you something to lean on throughout your uncertain quest to finding your true purpose. This is big and not to be taken lightly. YOU ARE IMPORTANT in this divine plan

Key points/checklist

CONCLUSION

In conclusion I pray that you have gained a better sense of your power! I hope that you can apply what you've read to part of your life to help aid you in becoming the best version of yourself. Please utilize the key points section. I encourage you to revisit chapters or to get a better understanding as well as be reminded of some of the exercises. Some people take longer than others to gather information and apply. Overall, I want the best for you, and I want you to want the same. I never would've thought the things I went through in life and overcame would be lessons for me to pass on my wisdom to others who will go through the same. I'm still getting lessons thrown my way, we all are but we can gain a better understanding the more we are in tune into what we truly are! Now, what's more powerful than you!?

Made in the USA
Columbia, SC
16 July 2024